M.F.K. FISHER'S PROVENCE

PLATE ONE — *La Rotunde, Cours Mirabeau*

M.F.K. FISHER'S

Provence

WITH 61 COLOR PHOTOGRAPHS BY

Aileen Ah-Tye

FOREWORD BY
LUKE BARR

COUNTERPOINT • BERKELEY, CALIFORNIA

Library of Congress Cataloging-in-Publication Data Is Available

Cover design by Kelly Winton
Interior design by Gopa & Ted2. Inc.

ISBN 978-1-61902-594-3

Counterpoint Press
2560 Ninth Street, Suite 318
Berkeley, CA 94710
www.counterpointpress.com

Printed in China
Distributed by Publishers Group West

10 9 8 7 6 5 4 3 2 1

For John Davidson

Contents

Simple Pleasures in Aix-en-Provence

W E SHOPPED morning, noon, and night in Provence—we shopped for croissants, baguettes, newspapers, and cigarettes, for tomatoes, peaches, string beans, strawberries, eggplants, mushrooms, and lettuce. We shopped for legs of lamb and chickens, for cubes of beef for stew, and for pork sausages. We shopped for butter and milk and cheese, and for honey and cases of wine and Badoit mineral water. We shopped for breakfast, lunch, and dinner, and then we started over again.

For basic provisions, we went into the village—our house was in tiny Puyricard, on the outskirts of Aix. The town had an old stone church next to the post office, three bakeries, a little Casino supermarket, a butcher, and a café with vaguely unfriendly, pastis-drinking middle-aged men, the kind that can be found in every French village. Sometimes they played *pétanque*.

I never did figure out which bakery had the best croissants, and it didn't matter, they were all good. We bought them eight or ten at a time: not too big, buttery but not overly rich, satisfyingly crunchy but still tender and elastic inside. At the newsstand we'd pick up the *International Herald Tribune* and *L'Équipe*, the sports tabloid. We got to know the mom, pop, and son who ran the supermarket and who did their best to help find what we needed, with mixed success (dried red-pepper flakes? ". . . Non," came the reply, heads shaking sadly). The butcher was hip and friendly, in his thirties but his close-cropped hair already going gray. His lamb chops were incredible.

And so it was that we developed a routine, a rhythm, a kind of easygoing daily schedule, loosely correlated to hunger and appetite. The main event was the farmers' market in downtown Aix. On the Place Richelme, under the shade of a canopy of tall plane trees, this was a farmers' market to end all farmers' markets. Not that it was very big, or particularly fancy, but it was idyllic; the market was busy from early morning until just after lunch, full of sturdy matrons pulling two-wheeled carts and parents pushing strollers, the hustle and flow of commerce. The vegetables were beautiful—densely colored peppers, eggplants, and tomatoes, fresh garlic, yellow string beans—and the fruits were even more beautiful—small, sweet strawberries, baskets of red currants, figs, and apricots, all sorts of peaches, nectarines, plums, and melons. One man sold goat cheeses, aged to different vintages, and honey; another had hams and salami, including a heavy and rectangular aged lonzo from Corsica. We sliced our pieces thin, so it would last longer.

I have every reason to love the market in the Place Richelme: I inherited a love for it, indeed, for Aix itself. My father lived here when he was a kid in 1959: my grandmother Norah Barr brought her three sons and rented a house not far from her sister, M.F.K. Fisher, who had rented a place just outside Aix with her two daughters. I grew up hearing

about this epic trip, and an earlier one in 1954—from my father and uncles, mostly, about the boat ride from California down through the Panama Canal and across the Atlantic; about learning French in school in Switzerland and then moving to France for the other half of the year, attending the same lycée Paul Cézanne had.

M.F. by this point was a well-established writer, and she recorded the trip in subsequent years—in 1964 in *Map of Another Town*, for example, a book about Aix. She described the "green light" that filtered through the plane trees above the market at Place Richelme in an essay for *The New Yorker* in 1966: "Perhaps some fortunate fish have known it, but for human beings it is rare to float at the bottom of the deeps and yet breathe with rapture the smells of all the living things spread out to sell in the pure, filtered, moving air."

Rereading her today, it's often striking how little has changed. Fifty years later, the market is precisely as she described it, minus the "ducklings bright-eyed in their crates" and other livestock. Then again, in many other ways Aix has also changed completely—and so what if it has? I'm not going to pretend to be nostalgic about 1959—hell, I was born in 1968. But on this trip I was accompanied by my father and my grandmother, and

I did want to see the city through their eyes—however momentarily, in whatever glancing, refracted way, to have a visceral sense of a past that lives on embedded in the present. But the strange thing is that's not what happened at all. Or at least not the only thing.

THE HOUSE WE RENTED came with a rabbit, and of course the kids loved him. He was plump and brown, and lived in a rather elegant wood-and-stone-framed cage underneath the fig tree. We fed him carrots, and joked about eating him for dinner.

Our bedrooms were on the second floor of the 300-year-old *mas*, a solidly constructed stone building covered in vines and with terra-cotta-tiled floors. The kitchen was simple and spare, and had a long, zinc-topped table at its center and a door that opened out onto the graveled courtyard. In the morning I would walk out, say hello to the rabbit, and sit on one of the rickety chairs at the rickety wood-slat table, or on a creaking canvas lounge chair under the enormous plane tree, and drink my coffee. Who was driving into town, and how many baguettes did we need?

The grounds were magnificent— sprawling lawns; olive, apple, plum, fig, and unruly cypress trees; lavender and rosemary bushes all over—the lavender positively thrumming with bees—white and dark pink laurel, grapevines, and potted lemon trees; a *pétanque* court, a ping-pong table, a fabulous and over- grown herb garden—dry, fragrant thyme and sage, basil, lemon verbena, and three varieties of rosemary—a pristine pool and a pool house with a chimneyed charcoal grill and a large dining table.

Some combination of the dry heat and the easy back-and-forth from inside to outside—the screenless doors and windows were always open, with warm breezes, children, and the occasional grasshopper making their way in and out of the house—reminded me of Califor- nia. My grandmother's house in Sonoma, the house I grew up loving, had a sim- ilarly overgrown and carelessly beauti- ful garden, a row of tall poplar trees, a scruffy lawn, and flower and vegetable plantings overlooking the Russian River and the Pacific Ocean. Inside were cats and a dog, threadbare Oriental carpets, a large kitchen, and endless evening bridge games. M.F.'s house in Glen Ellen was a little more formal, a thick-walled palazzo set back from the road overlooking a field of grapevines, but both of them epito- mized for me a sort of genteel, unpre- tentious, and yet highly sophisticated California style.

I always knew, of course, that our California life had a Provençal flavor, in the dishes my grandmother and great-aunt cooked, in the art hung on their walls. But it wasn't until I arrived that I really understood how much of my family's aesthetic and cultural DNA had its roots right here, in Aix.

Aix is a university town and former provincial capital, built around Roman baths and numerous churches. It has narrow cobblestoned streets leading through various plazas, and it's built on a slope. And so the town seems to carry you gently but persuasively down the hill and toward its center, at least when you enter, as we did, from the north side, which was where the road from Puyricard deposited us. The streets were lined with clothing stores, cafés, gift shops, and patisseries. One day my wife and I stopped to buy some Provençal dishes to replace the ones my grandmother bought back in the 50's and 60's and which I still used (they ended up in my kitchen a few years back), even though they were chipped and quite possibly full of lead, i.e., poisonous.

As I say, the town pulls you toward its heart, its grand central street, the Cours Mirabeau. With two tall rows of plane trees and a series of fountains and cafés, it makes you slow down and exhale. M.F. described the Cours this way: "It is a man-made miracle, perhaps indescribable, compounded of stone and water and trees, and to the fortunate it is one of the world's chosen spots for their own sentient growth." I'm not sure I experienced "sentient growth," but I wholeheartedly agree.

We ate dinner at Les Deux Garçons, the famous (and these days quite touristy) café on the Cours, a place M.F. spent hours watching the comings and goings, and never a place one came for the food, but rather for the ambience, as my grandmother pointed out.

Not far away, on a quiet street just off the Cours, we paid a visit—we paid our respects, I want to say—to the fountain of the Four Dolphins. This fountain was my grandmother and M.F.'s favorite, my father and his brothers and cousins' favorite: our family favorite, in other words. As advertised, the fountain consisted of four stone dolphins, smiling and cheerful but each with a slightly different expression, spouting thin streams of water into the basin below. "This fountain is great," said my father definitively, expressing neither a strictly aesthetic judgment nor simple, unbridled enthusiasm, but rather something more transcendent, a serious claim of affection, and one that he wanted us to share. (And which we did.)

He remembered the Four Dolphins so well from when he was 13, and here it was, 50 years later, and still wonderful.

But of course, some things do not survive—some things become unrecognizable. A few blocks away was the Hôtel Roi René, where we now thought we'd go for an after-dinner drink before heading back to the house. The Roi René was once *the* hotel in Aix, the epitome of elegance and so forth, the place where M.F. had stayed for weeks at a time in the early 50's, where she and my grandmother and the kids would check in every so often for a weekend in the late 50's, to take hot baths and order room service, and where my father remembers a sprawling suite with a balcony overlooking the Boulevard du Roi René, and watching the Tour de France whiz by below.

As we walked in we were confronted with a beige-and-pink color scheme and a collection of hyperbanal corporate furniture. The place had none of the glamour my dad and grandmother remembered—not an iota.

I LOVED THE GRAVEL in Provence: the sound of it under the wheels of the car in the potholed driveway, the expanse of it around our house, on the paths to the guest cottage and herb garden and swimming pool. There's something pleasantly austere about Provençal gravel—it has a calm, cooling effect, setting off the wild and abundant vegetation and the hot sun. At the restaurant Chez Thomé, tables were placed on gravel underneath the shade of the trees. This casual country place is another family favorite, up there with the Four Dolphins. We walked across the gravel to our table as cicadas chirped in the nearby fields.

When my grandmother and great-aunt lived here in '59, they both rented houses a few miles from Aix, M.F. along the Route du Tholonet, a winding road heading east out of town toward Le Tholonet, a small village in the shadow of Mont Sainte-Victoire. On the drive here, we'd tried in vain to spot the driveway to L'Harmas, the farmhouse she'd rented. It didn't matter—the road offered its own stunning dramas, curving through dry green hills and thickets of trees, Sainte-Victoire intimidating and stern in the distance. This is what's known as the Route Cézanne (he painted these scenes in the 1890's), and it still looks that way, like a painting.

Coming into the center of town, we passed by the imposing Château du Tholonet, where M.F. had rented an apartment above the stables in the mid 50's, and my grandmother and her sons had visited. Describing her mealtime routines, M.F. wrote: "There was always that little rich decadent tin of lark pâté in the cupboard if I grew bored, or we could stroll down past the great ponds under the plane trees to the deft, friendly welcome of the Restaurant Thomé and eat a grilled pullet or a trout meunière, and an orange baked à la norvégienne."

As for us, we ordered beautiful green salads with red currants, a bit of foie gras, warm cheese with a red pepper-and-garlic rémoulade, rabbit with a dried-fruit reduction, and *risotto aux fruits de mer*. I hesitate to write so hyperbolically, but I must say that it was a perfect lunch—perfect. Sitting under the trees in this unspeakably beautiful courtyard, at an informal table with my family and friends, I felt a connection to this place, and to Aix, that went beyond my own immediate experiences. I had come to find Aix, and found it was already in me, or to quote M.F. describing her arrival here all those years ago, "I was once more in my own place, an invader of what was already mine."

Luke Barr

PLATE TWO — *Olive Trees, by Les Baux*

PLATE THREE — *Red-Tiled Roofs, outside Aix-en-Provence*

PLATE FOUR — *Café Cat, Deux Garçons, Cours Mirabeau*

PLATE FIVE — *Lunch Break, Cours Mirabeau*

PLATE SIX — *Stairway, Hôtel de Caumont, Aix*

PLATE SEVEN — *Door, Hôtel de Panisse, Aix*

PLATE EIGHT — *Discarded Roses, Flower Market*

My Map

OFTEN IN THE SKETCH for a portrait, the invisible lines that bridge one stroke of the pencil or brush to another are what really make it live. This is probably true in a word picture too. The myriad undrawn unwritten lines are the ones that hold together what the painter and the writer have tried to set down, their own visions of a thing: a town, one town, this town.

Not everything can be told, nor need it be, just as the artist himself need not and indeed cannot reveal every outline of his vision.

There before us is what one human being has seen of something many others have viewed differently, and the lines held back are perhaps the ones most vital to the whole.

Here before me now is my picture, my map, of a place and therefore of myself, and much that can never be said adds to its reality for me, just as much of its reality is based on my own shadows, my inventions.

Over the years I have taught myself, and have been been taught, to be a stranger. A stranger usually has the normal five senses, perhaps especially so, ready to protect and nourish him.

Then there are the extra senses that function only in subconsciousness. These are perhaps a stranger's best allies, the ones that stay on and grow stronger as time passes and immediacy dwindles.

It is with the invisible ink distilled from all these senses, then, that I have drawn this map of a town, a place real in stone and water, and in the spirit, which may also be realer.

Aix-en-Provence

. . . Former capital of Provence; seat of an archbishopric since the fifth century, and of the departmental law courts and prison, and the schools of Law and Letters of the University of Aix-Marseille. . .

The town was founded in 123 BC by the Roman consul Sextius Calvinus, and was made into a prosperous colony by Julius Caesar. Between the fifth and twelfth centuries, it lost much of its political importance to the town of Arles, although it was once more made the capital in the twelfth century under the Counts of Provence.

During the fifteenth century, before joining France, it became the hub of European culture under the benevolent administration of King René and his two queens.

Le Guide Bleu: France

So here is the town, founded more than two thousand years ago by the brash Roman invaders, on much older ruins which still stick up their stones and artifacts. I was as brash a newcomer to it, and yet when I first felt the rhythm of its streets and smelled its ancient smells, and listened at night to the music of its many fountains, I said, "Of course," for I was once more in my own place, an invader of what was already mine.

Depending upon one's vocabulary, it is facile enough to speak of karma or atavism or even extrasensory memory. For me, there was no need to draw on this well of casual semantics, to recognize Aix from my own invisible map of it. I already knew where I was . . .

The town was put on its feet by a Roman whose elegant bathing place still splutters out waters, tepid to hot and slightly stinking . . .

This spa, more ancient than anyone who could possibly stay in it except perhaps I myself, is at the edge of the Old Town, at the head of the Cours Sextius, and more than one good writer has generated his own acid to etch its strange watery attraction.

Countless poems have been written too, in wine rather than acid, and countless pictures have been painted, about the healing waters and the ever-flowing fountains of the place. They will continue as long as does man, and the delicate iron balconies will cling to the rose-yellow walls, and if anyone else, from 200 BC to now, ever marked the same places on the map, in acid or wine or even tears, his reasons would not be mine. That is why Aix is what it is.

ON FACING PAGE:

PLATE NINE — *Roses, Pavillion de Vendôme*

Artful Pleasures

PLATE TEN — *Pain à Toasts*

THERE WERE at least three other pastry shops as good as hers, in a town perhaps more noted for them than any other in a country dedicated to the gastric hazards of almond paste, chestnuts soaked in sweet liqueurs, and chocolate in all its richest and most redolent forms . . .

. . . To a visitor the pageantry of the pastry shop windows was mysterious, exciting. It was plainly dictated by the supplies on hand, the new crop of almonds, the freshly preserved fruits like melons and cherries and figs, then the deep mysteries of all the different blends of chocolate at Christmas time, and the purity of Easter with white eggs and mimosa blossoms and sugar daffodils . . .

And there are always the calissons . . . I assured her once more that the little pointed ovals of artfully blended almond paste, were a superb confection, part pastry, part candy, light but rich, not cloying, haunting and delicate, old as the Romans or perhaps Jeanne the second queen of King René, a regal tidbit . . .

. . . There were two or three things there that I felt it almost a duty to enjoy while I could, like the little oblong slabs, each made in its own pan, of a kind of thin solid sponge cake called something like "paving blocks." In the other town, Dijon, they had been round and called Genoa bread. In Aix the taste and smell of them crept into my private map, so that even now I can eat one on the terrace of the shadow-café, while I wait for six o'clock and the end of the children's school day and a drink with them . . .

Often, after I left Aix the first time, I thought about the brilliant sights and smells of that rhythmic parade through the pastry shop windows. It was exciting. It was based on the main supplies of the strange rich dry land; the almonds, the colors of all the fruits and fishes, the spring floods of eggs and cream and syrups. Religion took it over, with pagan rituals behind the altars: spring, marriage, birth and rebirth, the miracles of Christmas and Easter.

PLATE ELEVEN — *Fanciful Breads*

. . . The shop always smelled right, not confused and stuffy but delicately layered: fresh eggs, fresh sweet butter, grated nutmeg, vanilla beans, old kirsch, newly ground almonds . . .

PLATE TWELVE — *Pots, Château de Sabran*

From the Deux Garçons I could see the windows of her shop. They were a blaze of brilliant fish shaped in replicas of all the mean, bright, fanged, horned, spikedy things that go into a real boullabaisse, painted on artful molds of pure almond paste, spilling from nets and from reed baskets onto the wide window shelf. Seaweeds shaped from tinted sugar caught them. Tiny mussels and urchins tangled in the shadows . . .

Was it for the Rites of Spring, the coming of the first strawberries, gleaming tiny fraises des bois looking more beautiful than possible in their little straw baskets, all made of sugar and vividly painted almond paste? . . .

. . . For me there never was the real reason for this annual invasion, for I never got any kind of calendar of these tides and rhythms. I followed them dumbly, perhaps as a fish follows the currents that push it here and there, and make it hungry one time and amorous the next and never more than protestingly wondering.

Main Street

PLATE THIRTEEN — *Before the Parade, Cours Mirabeau*

THE COURS MIRABEAU is the main street of Aix-en-Provence. It is less than half of a mile long (440 meters) and some hundred and twenty feet wide. It is bordered on either side by a double row of plane trees, growing in front of the straight façades of seventeenth- and eighteenth-century townhouses, most of them with shops or offices on the ground floor now. There are four fountains down the middle of the Cours' length, and . . .

. . . and it is impossible to continue writing of it in this informative vein.

The Cours has teased poets and painters with its ineffable allure for more than three hundred years, but words and lines and colors do not capture the reasons why it is beautiful and not pretty, serene and not soothing, and dignified yet gladsome all the year, even in the stripped austerity of winter.

It is probable that almost every traveler who has ever passed through Aix has been moved in some positive way by the view from one end of the Cours or the other, by the sounds of its fountains in the early hours, by the melodious play of the pure clear sunlight of Provence through its summer cave of leaves. Some of them have tried to tell of their bemused rapture, on canvas and sketch pads and on scratch-pads and even postcards, but they have never been satisfied.

It is a man-made miracle, perhaps indescribable, compounded of stone and water and trees, and to the fortunate it is one of the world's chosen spots for their own sentient growth.

Myself, for too few years I crossed it many times a day, and sat under its trees, and walked up and down it on both sides alone and with my children and now and then with friends, in sunlight and moonlight and rain and fog, and every time it was the first time, and I felt a kind of prickling under my skin and a tightening in my chest and belly and a kind of dazzling in my head and a generally excited stimulated moved sensation, like being in love.

PLATE FOURTEEN — *King René, Cours Mirabeau*

PLATE FIFTEEN — *La Rotunde, Cours Mirabeau*

The street was made in 1651, after Marie de Médicis brought from Italy to France the aristocratic pleasure of taking the air in public, either in carriages or on foot or in sedan chairs, instead of walking quietly in one's own gardens. It became at once the center of Aix, and so it has remained.

PLATE SIXTEEN — *Mime, Cours Mirabeau*

PLATE SEVENTEEN — *Under the Plane Trees*

Motor scooters and automobiles have replaced the chairs and open carriages that paraded during the cool of the evenings on the Cours of other days, but the delight of strolling its length at any time, in every season, has never ceased to charm, indeed almost to hypnotize whoever sets foot on its majestic length and width.

PLATE EIGHTEEN — *La Rotunde*

There are still four
fountains, the length
of the Cours, just as at
its beginning . . .

Compared to
the other fountains
of Aix, the Rotunde
is melodramatic,
overstated, brassy,
a trumpet call
with flutes . . .

In daylight La
Rotunde tosses out
its many plumes and
jets of water like the
breath of a hundred
spirited horses.

The houses that face each other across the double width of the Cours Mirabeau, and then over the tops of the plane trees from their attics, are one of the few remaining entities of the seventeenth and eighteenth centuries in European architecture, unbombed and unburned in spite of the hazards and crimes of progress.

PLATE NINETEEN — *Hôtel de Caumont*

. . . A few beautiful private apartments are still preserved, and the exquisite iron balconies of most of the houses, and then their staircases inside, are tenderly protected by their care-takers and the city and and the nation, so that students of all the arts may admire them.

PLATE TWENTY — *Hôtel de Gaillard d'Agoult*

At street level, the tone of the Cours has changed almost completely since it was first built as an aristocratic promenade . . . By now the Left Bank is an almost unbroken series of stores both great and small and mostly reputable, of open-air cafés for every class of people, of agencies for every need.

PLATE TWENTY-ONE — *Calissons d'Aix*

In Aix, and I presume in every other respectable town of France, both great and small, cafés are known by the company they keep, and in one way or another the towns are known by their cafés. For most of this century, Aix has been for itself and its visitors the Deux Garçons, the Café of the Two Waiters.

PLATE TWENTY-TWO — *Lamp, Deux Garçons*

PLATE TWENTY-THREE — *Mirrors, Deux Garçons*

PLATE TWENTY-FOUR — *Zinc Bar, Deux Garçons*

It is two large rooms, elegant in a deliberately faded style. The larger, which gives now onto the Cours Mirabeau through its door and two big windows, is long, with a looming old zinc bar across its far end, where the waiters fill their orders except for liqueurs and spirits, which are dispensed carefully at the high cashier's desk near the two public telephone booths. The main part of this room is mirrored, with woodwork painted dimly in gold and black . . .

PLATE TWENTY-FIVE — *Student Room, Deux Garçons*

In the room to the left, which also gives onto the Cours, the elegant old décor is simpler . . . Students sit there, as they always have, or rare tourists who do not know that they are intruding on the cabalistic rituals of beer and Gauloises Bleues.

PLATE TWENTY-SIX — *Charlotte, Law Student, Deux Garçons*

PLATE TWENTY-SEVEN — *George, Deux Garçons*

. . . the waiters can be as firm as any Mother Superior . . .

Across the whole generous façade of the Deux Garcons stretches a terrace filled with little marble-topped tables, and dozens of green chairs. In summer it is deeply shaded by the double row of towering plane trees of the Left Bank of the Cours. In winter it catches all the thin pure sunlight that falls through their naked branches. In the spring the light is incredibly dappled and of the color of a fine greenish wine from the Moselle. Sometimes in late autumn after a rainy wind there are only a few eccentrics who still sit there, to watch the golden leaves plastered against the shining black pavement of the street.

PLATE TWENTY-EIGHT — *Terrace, Deux Garçons*

PLATE TWENTY-NINE — *Pavillion de Vendôme*

Rose-Yellow Façades

I COULD COUNT on two or three walks across the Old Town to see Anne and Mary as they got out of school at noon, and then in the late afternoon. We would go to the Deux Garçons or the Glacier together for an ice or sandwich: that would take two hours in almost every day.

Then coffee and reading in bed would use another half-hour or so each morning.

Slow roamings took another two hours or three . . . drifting along the streets to listen to the fountains and ruminate upon the proportions, of the rose-yellow façades, three-to-six-to-nine, and the cornices, and the corner Madonnas, and the caryatids turning breasts and backs, male and sometimes female, to my gaze; and the open markets in three squares and occasionally along the narrow streets; and the libraries and museums: all these accustomed me to my invisibility.

. . . Talk is as steady as the fountains themselves, in Aix.
It goes on everywhere, sometimes noisy but seldom harsh . . .

PLATE THIRTY-ONE — *Tête-á-Tête at the Market*

PLATE THIRTY-TWO — *Aix Food Market*

A personal map, one like mine of Aix, has places on it which no printer could indicate, for they are clear only as a smell, or a sound, or a moment of light or dark . . .

There is the Aix smell, made up of the best air I have ever breathed, purified by all the fountains and the tall trees and the stalls piled with sweet fresh vegetables in the open markets. I feel quite sure that if I could be teleported, blind, to a dozen places I have known, that smell would be the truest one to my inner nose . . .

We seemed to grow like water-flowers under the growing buds
of plane trees, in the flowing tides of the street.

PLATE THIRTY-THREE — *By Café de l'Horloge*

The Tour des Augustins is very worn now and the fine ironwork belfry is silent, but the color of it in the sunset is deathless.

PLATE THIRTY-FOUR — *Tour des Augustins*

In the Country

I DID LIE in the meadow in the penetrating Provençal sun, and I did drink teas brewed from herbs picked that morning by my children, and I even lay in baths redolent of branches of fresh thyme . . . I let the hot sun and the meadow smells soothe me.

. . . One day we came in from the country with some sprays of almond blossoms . . . There was much talk about the unseasonable warmth, the great freeze of February 2 . . . ah, the dead olive trees, the almonds, the live oaks . . . and then the freeze of last April 30, which took two-thirds or three-quarters or five-eighths of the wine this year . . .

And then we went into the hotel and divided our branches . . . Anne put one branch in her room, and I stuck the other two in a jar of deep blue anemones by my desk. In the last bright light coming over the yellow and rose tiles of the rooftops, it seemed probably the most beautiful posy of my life.

I thought I should mention this in my invisible notes on the secret map . . .

PLATE THIRTY-SIX — *Lavender*

PLATE THIRTY-SEVEN — *Mas de Bonnet de la Roche*

All the windows of the simple pleasant house were wide open, a wonderful feeling for us after the winter in a hotel, and the walls were white plaster and the good furniture was dark with age and shining with wax, and the floors were of red square tiles. In other words, it was the kind of Provençal mas that I most love.

PLATE THIRTY-EIGHT — *Window, Mas de Bonnet de la Roche*

Sound of the Place

Exposition
Musée Granet, Musée des Tapisseries,
Pavillon de Vendôme

PLATE THIRTY-NINE — *Poster, Aix Music Festival*

AIX HAS BEEN called "the city of fountains and music," and the two are synonymous in it.

Summers, during the Festival, the whole town quivers to the sounds, in the open air of cloisters and courtyards, of violins and flutes and voices, and above them rises always the indescribably soft steady music from at least fourteen public fountains and uncounted murmuring basins hidden in gardens and inner courts.

Late at night the year around, and even during the midday hours in summer when all else sleeps, a person seeking it can hear water flowing and falling somewhere nearby, and then walk on a little to the magic radius of another and yet another fountain, rather as in the Tivoli in Copenhagen one can stroll from orchestra to orchestra without ever hearing the various sounds conflict and snarl.

PLATE FORTY — *Violins*

I would forever hear the little mandolin, plucked in the orchestra pit while onstage Don Giovanni pretended to play to the silent mockery of an inn where his mock-love listened. And I knew in a fine positive way that I could nevermore walk any street in the whole real world without hearing, somewhere up from the immediate sounds, the quiet music of the fountains of Aix.

PLATE FORTY-ONE — *Don Giovanni's Costume*

PLATE FORTY-TWO — *Four Dolphins*

Each quarter in Aix has its main public fountain, to which it is unquestioningly loyal. It is always the clearest, purest, most beneficent water to its users, in this or that particular source, which springs up through the subterrain as if through a miraculous filter, here warm and fumy, there icy-sweet.

PLATE FORTY-THREE — *Fountain, Place d'Albertas*

ON FACING PAGE:

PLATE FORTY-FOUR — *Boar Fountain*

PLATE FORTY-FIVE — *Vieux Port*

PLATE FORTY-SIX — *Marseillaise*

Marseille

PLATE FORTY-SEVEN — *Stern, Tall Ship*

A TRUE KARMIC FORCE is supposed to build up its strength through centuries of both evil and good, in order to prevent its transmigration into another and lesser form, and this may well explain why Marseille has always risen anew from the ashes of history. There seems to be no possible way to stamp it out. Julius Caesar tried to, and for a time felt almost sure that he had succeeded.

Calamities caused by man's folly and the gods' wrath, from the plagues ending in 1720 to the invasions ending in the 1940s, have piled it with rotting bodies and blasted rubble, and the place has blanched and staggered, and then risen again.

It has survived every kind of weapon known to European warfare, from the ax and arrow to sophisticated derivatives of Chinese gunpowder, and it is hard to surmise that if a nuclear blast finally leveled the place, some short dark-browned men and women might eventually emerge from a few dark places, to breed in the salt marshes that would gradually have revivified the dead waters around the Old Port . . .

Meanwhile, Marseille lives, with a unique strength that plainly scares less virile breeds. Its people are proud of being "apart," and critics mock them for trying to sound even more Italianate than they are, trying to play roles for the tourists: fishermen ape Marcel Pagnol's *Marius* robustly; every fishwife is her own *Honorine*.

PLATE FORTY-EIGHT — *Scene From Pagnol*

The Quai des Belges is
the shortest of the Port's
three shores, at the head,
the land end, of the little
harbor. Like all centers of
life past and present,
it is concentrated . . .
with careful room for
the fishermen, to chug
in six or seven mornings
a week to set up their
rickety tables in the casual
market that strings out
along the wide sidewalk.

PLATE FORTY-NINE — *Marseillaise*

The native women
of Marseille, the ones
who are unmistakably
of this place and no
other that I have seen
or read about, are short
and trimly wide . . .

As girls they have
a slim beauty that soon
passes into what they
will be for the rest of
their lives . . .

They may develop paunches, the tidy kind that look made of steel, and among the lot of them there is never a snub nose, but instead the kind that grows stronger and beakier with time. Their arms and legs stay shapely enough, thanks surely to hard work, and their skins become like well-soaped leather, thanks perhaps to good olive oil and garlic and an occasional pastis, all taken by mouth in daily doses. (Tomatoes are also thanked for continuing their female vigor, according to many of their mates . . .)

PLATE FIFTY — *Marseillaise*

In all the Marseillaises seem almost a part of their craggy land, like the thick trunks of the most ancient olive trees on the hills behind the city. And still they are from the sea, so that they smell of salt, and of what they eat and what they work with, but never of old sweat.

PLATE FIFTY-ONE — *Fresh Catch*

During the Market hours there, men sold their catches, too, but it was the women who dominated, at least in decibels. The men simply stood behind their piles of gleaming sardines, slithery small octupi, long eels trying to get back into the dirty Port water, greyish-pink shrimps hopping within their pyramids of myriad brothers.

PLATE FIFTY-TWO —— *Fisherman, Quai des Belges*

PLATE FIFTY-THREE — *Fish Heads, Quai des Belges*

They smiled and chatted in a detached way as they scooped the catch into newspaper cones, or whacked something into immobility for its last ride toward the kitchen, but they seemed poised for escape from all the selling end of their game. That was for the women. Once the fish got to shore, the men were set to head out to sea again . . . les pescadous.

Food of Artemis

PLATE FIFTY-FOUR — *Tomatoes at the Market*

I T HAS BEEN said, and rightly, that a tomato of Provence tastes different from that grown from the same seed in another soil and air. It will have a pungency, an earthy savor, and a smell that are robust but not coarse. It makes understandable at once, without words, why the men of the South of France know that the reason their women ("strong, wild, fertile," they have been called) are more lastingly seductive than others is that they are fed from the cradle on the local love apples.

These fruits, sliced fresh from the gardens, cooked into every conceivable dish, made into thick pastes for winter sustenance; alone or with a little olive oil; stewed, baked, grilled in countless ways: tomatoes in Marseille stand alone or blend happily with eggs, fish, meats.

They are true kitchen stalwarts, like the human females who feed on them.

This same salty vitality is everywhere else in Provence, as far as I can see. Women, tomatoes, children and men, herbs and trees . . . and sheep and the small black fighting bulls: they all have it.

The rice of the Camargue, for instance . . . one of the most unusual and delicious grains I ever tasted, hard and strongly salted.

The wines . . . have a dryness that makes them truly "sand wines," sprung up almost as fast as the rice before them, and the marsh grasses before the rice, on the edge of the Mediterranean.

All this durable strength, this mysterious saltiness is what gives the food as well as the wine of the Marseille a zest that I have never known anywhere else.

PLATE FIFTY-FIVE — *Reed Gatherer, Camargue*

PLATE FIFTY-SIX — *Camargue. Horses*

As an almost professional ghost, I have developed a fairly dependable nose for good public eating places, from the most stylish-but-honest to the lowliest-but-honorable. I know that nearly all French towns can boast of one kind or the other, and that the big cities are filled with them. but for me Marseille remains the chosen magical Mysterious One. And I think it is because of the peculiar liveliness of what grows behind it on the ancient soil, and especially what swims and creeps and slithers at its watery gates.

PLATE FIFTY-SEVEN — *Slithery Blue Eels*

PLATE FIFTY-EIGHT — *Fish, Quai des Belges*

There is no doubt about it: freshly caught fish, scaly or in the shell have a different flavor and texture and smell there than in any other port of the world. The flavor is intense and assertive, no matter how delicate: a loup, for instance, will remain its own self even when grilled over dry fennel leaves and then flamed with an extra douse of Pernod. Texture is fine or coarse or succulent or crisp, depending on whether one eats a fresh sardine, a filet of tuna, a raw mussel. And the smell is so pure that it is as heady as the first breath from a dark winery cellar just hosed down —or from a silent printing pressroom if one reacts as I do to good ink and paper.

PLATE FIFTY-NINE — *Mending Nets, Quai des Belges*

The Mediterranean has fed us for so long that it is unlikely even current human stupidities of pollution and destruction will stop its generosity.

As we learn respect instead of carelessness, its fish will swim more healthily than ever, and its shells will form closer to the shorelines again, and the salt-sweet weeds will wave lushly for the picking.

And meanwhile there will probably be places, as now, where we can smell the tonic freshness of a stand of mollusks on their cool grass, and choose a fish to be poached or broiled while we pick wee snails with a sharp pin from their shells. Even strangers in a port like Marseille will let their noses guide them to such pleasures . . .

PLATE SIXTY — *Fisherman, Quai des Belges*

I wonder if I'll ever be there, once more, to look down on the Old Port, and drain the shell of every oyster on my plate, and then perhaps eat a piece of orange tart.

I wonder if I want to. It is tiring, sometimes, to play the phoenix . . . even in that salt-sweet air.

Artemis, help me!

PLATE SIXTY-ONE — *Notre Dame de la Garde Basilica*

AFTERWORD:

A Short History

YOU CAN IMAGINE my feelings when I confronted this sign tacked to the front door of M.F.K. Fisher's Glen Ellen home some years back: "Friends: Ring and come in. Foes: Enter (any old way). I mean this . . . MFK." A UPI photographer on assignment, I was holding a paper bag of croissants purchased from the local bakery. I felt apprehensive before, but now I was terrified. I had good company, however. Veteran reporter John Leighty, assigned a feature story on the publication of her *Dubious Honors*, and John Davidson, my husband and our driver who wasn't going to pass up a chance to meet the celebrated M.F.K. Fisher. The three of us were led into her kitchen-dining room, passing by a book of Matisse prints on an easel and seeing before us a terrace with wide, sunny views of the Sonoma hills.

In a moment, in walks Fisher, a tall woman with hair sinuously pinned up, the cheekbones of a Hepburn and a smile directed at me, "Will my eyebrows do?" "She's asking me?" I thought, looking into a pair of appraising eyes and the most expressive eyebrows I had ever seen. "They're fine," I assured her, happy to be made a friend, not a foe.

Mrs. Fisher proved to be as gracious and unpretentious an interview subject as you could want, telling Leighty: "I'm 80, still working and my books are all in print. It's an odd one . . . it's embarrassing." She loved to talk and was a good listener. So we relaxed, buoyed by our conversation, touching on Van Gogh's love for the colors of Provence, good writing in Hemingway's *A Moveable Feast* and which famous writer to invite for a meal.

On subsequent visits we learned that Mrs. Fisher cultivated many interests: music, opera, painting, travel. She was well aware of who the current writers were and listened to them on tape. The books on her shelves intrigued me—books on gypsies, witches, France and food. I remember a papier-mâché bull she had sitting in her bedroom, something I secretly coveted. It could have been sculpted by Picasso. It had that exact touch of whimsical humor which was a Fisher trademark.

She understood that these pleasures nourished the soul. And when a hip operation prevented her from visiting Grasse with her nephew, she encouraged us to see Provence for ourselves. I had read her travel classic *Two Towns in Provence* and thought it contained some of the best prose I had ever read. Her "celtic eye for detail" had a special appeal for a photographer. Always the sensualist, Fisher's description of the sights and smells belonging to an Aix bakery shop window is her Platonic ideal of a bakery shop to be found anywhere in France. The shops "always smelled right, not confused and stuffy but delicately layered: Fresh eggs, fresh sweet butter, grated nutmeg, vanilla beans, old kirsch, newly ground almonds." Then, there is her portrayal of the sounds of Aix's fountains, interleaved with the music of Mozart during the town's famous festival, which left her bedazzled, so that she returned again and again to Provence.

This was the beginning of my sev-eral trips to Aix and Marseille. I laugh when I reread a letter I wrote after my first trip to Marseille. "The eels and the prickly rascasse were 'exotique' to my San Francisco eyes, the smells as pungent as you can get, and . . . miracle of all miracles . . . the men and women on the docks were exactly as you described them."

It was very exciting to share my photos upon our return. She was delighted when I first brought back *Pain à Toasts,* the photo of a Aix bakery window with breads stylized in fanciful shapes, and, later, photos of the Aix countryside with its red-tiled roofs and the summer scent of lavender, where Fisher had "let the hot sun and meadow smells soothe me." Thus began a collaboration on a book project that continued until her death in 1992, when Robert Lescher, her then literary trustee and longtime agent, became my listening post as I struggled to formulate these extracts of her writing.

I approached Mrs. Fisher's prose as one would music. The theme and counter-theme is the comparison between Aix, the stylish university town, the site of an international music festival and the former capital of Provence, with the port of Marseille and its rougher but enduring culture which Fisher so brilliantly encapsulated when they paired Fisher's two memoirs *Map of Another Town* and *A Considerable Town* to become *Two Towns in Provence.*

My prelude consists of her short, lyrical opening passages from *Map of Another Town* when Fisher sketches her "map of Provence" in "invisible ink distilled from all these senses."

The conclusion is when Fisher pleads for help from the god of Artemis: will she return to "look down on the old Port, and drain the shell of every oyster on my plate . . . It is tiring, sometimes to play the Phoenix . . . even in that salt-sweet air. Artemis, help me!"

Underlying her prose is the story she weaves into the background of her two books, the story of an American woman living in Provence with her two young daughters where they "seemed to grow like water-flowers under the greening buds of the plane trees, in the flowing tides of the streets." It is the quality of Fisher's writing that inspires a similar "ornery passion" in my photography, especially when it came to capturing her sense of place. And I've taken another page from Fisher's book, remembering her terse reply when asked by Leighty to consider her accomplishments in life: "'What a question,' she said witheringly, 'existing with any style, panache or aplomb is hard enough.'" I like that.

Acknowledgments

MY THANKS to John Leighty, the news writer who indelibly captured the character and personality of Mrs. Fisher in his UPI interview.

Cecily Gloppe was my intrepid guide to the mysteries of Aix. In her red Peugeot, we scoured the countryside for photos to find the antique copper pots used for the cover.

A gentleman of the old school, Robert Lescher, my agent and friend, saw me through completion of the text and layout, and obtained permission for the text from Map of Another Town. Bob was my touchstone for all things literary until his unexpected death.

Linda Meyerriecks, president of PhotoShepherd and picture editor for National Geographic for over forty years, supplied the grit and expertise to move on. Thank you, Bob Krist, National Geographic photographer, for recommending Linda and mentoring me from the beginning.

My thanks to Marsha and Patrick Moran for their encouragement, and especially to Marsha for putting in a good word for me with Kennedy Friede Golden, Mrs. Fisher's daughter and co-trustee of her literary estate along with Michael Carlisle, of Inkwell Management.

Sharon Cohen-Powers, layout artist, mastered working with Blurb software to produce a beautiful book mockup.

On the strength of her mockup, Michael recommended me to Jack Shoemaker, the editorial director of Counterpoint Press. My thanks to Michael for his support and to Hannah Schwartz, his assistant, for help in obtaining permission for the text from A Considerable Town.

Kennedy encouraged Luke Barr, her cousin and author of Provence: 1970, to write his marvelous foreword. His warm memories of his family's trips to Aix and Marseille add a much valued perspective. Thank you, Kennedy and Luke.

Peter Mayle wrote a wonderful Salon review of Mrs. Fisher's *Two Towns in*

Provence. Thank you, Peter, for your permission to publish an excerpt.

My thanks to Claire Shalinsky, Counterpoint's publicist, whose energy and enthusiasm make my "assignments," palatable, challenging and productive.

Thank you, Joseph Goodale, Counterpoint's administrative assistant, for proofreading the whole book, your follow up on the author's query, and attending to all the details that keep Counterpoint running smoothly.

Jack Shoemaker is my dream editor. He has the gift of drawing the best from me, to nudge me gently in the right directions and to be direct when required. This may only partially explain why he's known as a legendary editor.

Kelly Winton, Counterpoint's design manager, together with the designers at Gopa & Ted2, produced the inside "look" and designed the cover, a design concept that suits Mrs. Fisher to a T; that is, elegant and classy.

Ann Guilfoyle, founder of AGPix, introduced me to the world of photo books. Through her, I developed a keen appreciation. Thank you, Ann.

My husband, John Davidson, is my key sounding board and confidante who's accompanied me throughout the whole journey to publication.

And, finally, thank you Marilyn Cohen for being the wise counselor that you are.